Train of Thought is a Branch Line *Excursion*

Published by New Writing North

ISBN 978-0-9930588-5-1

New Writing North

3 Ellison Terrace

Newcastle upon Tyne

NE1 8ST

www.newwritingnorth.com

New Writing North 3166037 Registered charity number 1062729

NEW WRITING
NORTH

TRAIN OF THOUGHT

Words

MICHAEL CHAPLIN

Drawings

BIRTLEY ARIS

Birtley Aris Michael Chaplin

Branch Line

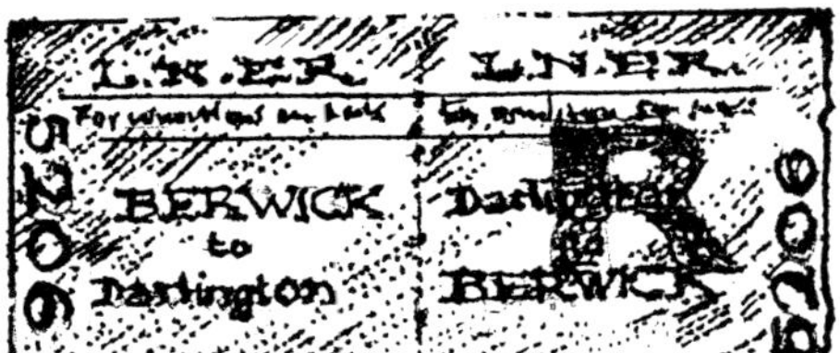
L.N.E.R.
L.N.E.R.
BERWICK
to
Darlington
BERWICK
Third Class
5206
5206

The Library is quiet, even more than usual. Outside the front door Westgate Road is silent, free of traffic. Outside at the back, the Station is also quiet.

In this coronavirus spring of 2020, everywhere in the city of Newcastle is quiet, apart from its two large hospitals. But we all hope, not for too long...

In times past and to come, sometimes as you sit in the great library of the Literary and Philosophical Society of Newcastle, you slowly become aware that other lives are going on out there. In the outside world.

This disconcerting revelation usually happens when there are few people inside, shortly after opening perhaps. Noises begin gently to impinge on your consciousness: metallic rattling, an occasional mechanical hoot, the distorted amplified sound of the human voice. It's a rather comforting reminder that while you are ensconced in the enclosed world created by some writer, many people out there are rushing around the country at speed and passing through one of the architectural marvels of the railway age, the Central Station, with its elegant *porte cochère* entrance and sweetly curving train shed in iron, stone and glass. Not just that, there's the warm realisation that its guiding spirits – Robert and George Stephenson – also had a bit to do with the creation of the Library itself.

For many reasons I am a child of the railway age – and perhaps now is the time to reflect on the journeys I have taken in my life.

One of my earliest memories is of being taken by my father from my grandparents' little pit house in Ferryhill to the side of a railway 100 yards away. A wooden fence stood between us and perhaps a dozen separate tracks. We waited. I noticed that the bottom rail of the fence jutted out towards me, so I put my left foot on it and leaned forward with my arms on the top rail. Then my dad tapped my shoulder and pointed south to a distant plume of smoke.

'See? It's coming,' he said.

Before I knew what was what the train was upon us with the roaring of moving parts and the maniacal shrieking of its whistle. We were

enveloped in a squall of hurricane proportions. I lost my hat and it seemed my wits. Then it was gone and Dad and I began to laugh…

A few years later, when I was 9, my Ferryhill grandmother died. Increasingly frail, she and my grandfather had come to live with my family in our Newcastle home. As the end approached, I was sent away to my other grandparents in Shildon and it was there one Sunday morning I was told Nana had passed away. I didn't know how to respond – but certainly didn't cry - and was soon running down a cinder track with my friend Bruce to the town's tiny station, giddy with excitement, for that day expresses were being diverted through it while engineering works were carried out on the main-line. We reached the track, climbed a fence, dropped onto the sloping roof of a wooden hut, got out the *ABC of British Locomotives* and waited. To our right was a tunnel and it was from that direction we first heard a noise – a low rumble, as if from the bowels of the earth, rising in pitch and volume, until the beast emerged from its lair with a towering column of black smoke. Bruce and I stood up, as if in the presence of royalty, for this was a queen of the line, the A4 Pacific locomotive 60003, with elegant sloping front and the euphonious name *Sir Andrew K. McCosh*. As it passed, the driver poked his capped head from the cab, smiled and pulled again on the whistle, and it was only now, with a hiss of steam and clatter of wheels, that the tears of loss unaccountably came.

There's an almost overwhelming temptation to write nostalgically about railways, especially those of the steam age, but there's far more to them than sentiment. They opened up the world in an unprecedented way, turning the Industrial Revolution into a social revolution that transformed this and many other countries. And it all started here by the Tyne. Railways began as waggon ways to transport coal to the ships carrying them to market, with the horse as motive power. There were nine on Tyneside by 1660 and they were so synonymous with the northern coalfield they came to be known as 'Newcastle roads'. The birth of steam-driven railways represented a huge leap forward and being as they are an amalgam of separate components - engine, track, rolling stock, which all required gradual development - they had many midwives. But the cleverest hands belonged to our own George Stephenson, obstreperous, self-educated genius from Wylam on Tyne. He had a brilliant knack of developing other people's ideas, shaking them till they worked and overcoming every obstacle, from exploding boilers to lawyers who mocked his accent. The heart of his world-changing enterprise was the Forth Banks works just across the tracks from the Lit and Phil. Here in the 1820s *Locomotion* was built for the Stockton and Darlington Railway and *Rocket* for the Liverpool and Manchester. By 1850 the railways had penetrated every corner of the British Isles. Many of the resulting breakthroughs were made by Stephenson and his followers, including Robert. Little wonder a railway historian has described the North-East as the Silicon Valley of its day.

Of the many effects of this transport revolution perhaps the greatest was on the lives of the common people. Before railways came along, horse-drawn coaches were so expensive the masses hardly moved at all and when they had to, they walked. Thomas Bewick, wood-engraver of this parish, once decided to visit friends in the Lake District and so walked there, then felt the urge to see Scotland and promptly strolled off to Edinburgh.

My own great-great grandfather set out one day with his wife and five children from their Suffolk home to seek work in the new industries of the north and didn't stop walking until he reached the first pit, in Shildon. Trains changed all that. Cheap 3rd class tickets ensured that industrial workers could soon enjoy, among many benefits, family excursions to the seaside and fresh fish however far inland they lived. From the beginning railways were the most democratic of transports, a shared experience for all, including me...

My first experience of rail travel was in 1953, when I was two. The whole family – my Mam Rene and Dad Sid, older sister Gillian and brother Chris – embarked on the six-hour journey from Ferryhill's little station to the grand terminal of King's Cross. The train had no connecting aisle, being divided into separate compartments.

At York Dad jumped off to buy a newspaper and cigarettes but didn't reappear before the train pulled out, nor at any of the many other stops, to the growing anxiety of my mother. Sid had tickets, money and knowledge of how precisely to travel onwards to our new home in Essex. At King's Cross Rene walked along the platform with her fractious children, anxiously rehearsing a speech to the ticket collector, when she saw her husband leaning against some railings with an insouciant smile. Family legend suggests he didn't wear it for long…

Almost every house I've occupied in almost 70 years has been by a railway. Indeed my life has been more or less defined by one in particular, the East Coast mainline. It's true I lived for a few years in a little box beside the track carrying electric trains back and forth between Liverpool Street and Southend and another 15 overlooking a stretch of London Underground's District Line a few stops from its Wimbledon terminus. But it was hard to get excited about these prosaic branches of the railway family, though from my study window in Southfields I did enjoy watching another kind of commuter on the Tube trackside – foxes loping towards town in the morning and back again in the afternoon. No, from childhood it was always the London to Edinburgh route that, well, floated my boat. As a boy lying in bed in Jesmond Vale the *whuff-whuff* of steam locos crossing Byker Bridge as they climbed away from the Tyne often lulled me to sleep. Forty years later I found myself living at the destination of many of those trains, in Edinburgh. In summer I would open my study window and hear a lilting female voice from nearby Haymarket, announcing imminent departures for points further north, if not the enchanted fictional halt of Glenbogle, the setting of many television scripts I wrote in those years. My favourite announcement was for the Fife Circle line, 'calling at Dalmeny, North Queensberry, Inverkeithing, Dalgety Bay, Aberdour, Burntisland, Kinghorn, Kirkcaldy, Glenrothes, Cardenden, Lochgelly, Cowdenbeath, Dunfermline Town, Rosyth, Inverkeithing, North Queensferry and Dalmeny…' This euphonious poem of place got under my skin so much I eventually wrote a radio play inspired by it, in which two old men – train driver and High Court judge – rattle around the Kingdom of Fife and discover they are actually half-brothers. Both parts were played by that master of disguise Stanley Baxter, who himself did a lot of travelling between Scotland and London, though coming from Glasgow he travelled on the West Coast route, poor man.

Now living once more in Newcastle, until the present interruption I'd take the London train maybe once a month. I couldn't begin to count the number of trips I've made on this line over the years – hundreds and hundreds – but I do know that if I was somehow teleported onto a train in mid-journey, it would only take a couple of minutes before the topography told me where I was. In my London years, I came north for family parties, holidays by the sea, play rehearsals and openings at Live Theatre, countless Newcastle matches and the occasional funeral. When my father died, the train crawled north, the rattle of the wheels a song of grief. But usually the journey is a transport of delight. One looks at the English landscape through a rectangular frame and the sense of cinema is enhanced when the traveller considers that one is as powerless to intervene in what one sees as James Stewart in *Rear Window*. This constantly changing panorama reminds the viewer that England remains a green and pleasant land, but as the miles click off, everything gets grander. Leaving London, we pass over Hertfordshire's curiously named River Mimram, via two sluggish Ouses, a Trent with several channels and a blackened Don to the holy trinity of Tees, Wear and Tyne. It's the same with the trackside progression of cathedrals: the minsters of Doncaster and York are an improvement on Peterborough but suffer by comparison with the matchless grandeur of Durham, perched on its rock. And finally to Newcastle...

To travel hopefully is a better thing than to arrive, said Robert Louis Stevenson, who crossed America by train in 1879. Perhaps he was thinking of his destination, Los Angeles (of which Gertrude Stein famously remarked, 'There is no *there* there), a hymn or dirge-like psalm to the motor-car. But one can't accuse the great gorge of the Tyne with its dizzy procession of bridges of such visual and spiritual emptiness, though Queen Victoria

TROP

may not have agreed. She travelled north in 1850 to open John Dobson's great station but was apparently sent a hotel bill by the city fathers for the privilege. Forever afterwards, en route to Balmoral and back, she lowered the blinds as the royal train passed through the smoky city that had so grievously insulted her. Strangely enough Arnold Bennett pulled the same stunt whenever he travelled through the Five Towns of the Potteries, the landscape that inspired his best work and made his reputation and fortune. Why? Disgust or guilt?

On these journeys to and from London, I sometimes reflect on the contribution of railways to our culture. Think of the books – everything from Graham Greene's *Stamboul Train* and Agatha Christie's *Murder on the Orient Express* to Dickens' *Dombey and Son*, the complete works of WH Awdry and Trollope's *Barchester Chronicles*, which aren't about trains but were more or less written entirely on them. In poetry we've Larkin's *Whitsun Weddings*, more Betjeman than you could wave a green flag at and that most evocative of opening lines: Yes, I remember Adlestrop...

In music, there's *Chattanooga Choo-Choo* and *Last Train to San Fernando*, as well as the heavyweight majesty of Honegger's *Pacific 231* and Steve Reich's haunting *Different Trains*, as well Paul Simon's beautiful song *Homeward Bound,* written early morning in 1965 at Widnes Station as he waited for a train to take him back to his girlfriend in London. In film there's a long list of wonderful movies that present the rich diversity of human experience, beginning with the short and prosaic *The Arrival Of A Train* of 1897; war films like *The Train and Von Ryan's Express*; thrillers like *From Russia With Love, Murder On The Orient Express* and *The Taking of Pelham 123*, and Hitchcock's trio of *The 39 Steps*, *The Lady Vanishes* and *Strangers On A Train*; comedies like Buster Keaton's *The General* and Ealing Studios' *The Titfield Thunderbolt*; and the, well, sheer poetry of Auden's *Night Mail.* Movies about the culture of the motor-car tend to be rather bleaker: *Thelma and Louise* doesn't end well, nor Spielberg's reputation-making *Duel*. Often the car is seen as a signifier for the dystopian hell of modern life, as for instance of *Crash*, two films of the same name by David Cronenberg and Paul Haggis.

In real life there's nothing on trains to match the nihilistic aggression of road-rage, apart from occasional disagreements about the use of a mobile phone. In my experience, people almost always behave like civilised beings and the vignettes on view are colourful. I once heard a black and white shirted football fan debate Karl Marx with a Civil Service mandarin working a piece of embroidery, a train guard recite Spike Milligan poems and an hilariously inebriated stage Scotsman serenade his carriage with songs from the shows. Perhaps a railway carriage is what anthropologists call a 'liminal zone' – a place where the otherwise strict rules prohibiting social intercourse with strangers are relaxed. Certainly, your average train provides a fascinating snapshot of contemporary Britons, their dress, modes of speech, conversational tics, reading matter and raw emotions. Over the years I've witnessed volcanic rows and filthy joke competitions; once interrupted coitus when opening an unlocked toilet door and more than once been moved by the tears of solitary women as they contemplated some loss. I've glimpsed the rich and famous, from the late Tony Benn to Newcastle's own Peter Beardsley and once encountered Hugh Grant and Jemima Khan wearing worried frowns as they realised they were a train length from their first-class comfort zone. Many people seem to prefer the collective ethic of railways to the individualism of the car, though commuters might disagree. One of my favourite pieces of railway literature is Roger Green's *Notes From Overground,* an aria to the servitude of the commuter which misquotes Rousseau's dictum thus: 'Man is born free, but is everywhere in trains.' But if it hadn't been for Green's daily grind I'd never have known that some inspired British Rail functionary once named the network's freight wagons after various forms of sea life: grampus, dogfish, haddock, ling, lamprey. I haven't spotted them for years now but then fish stocks are declining everywhere, even on the railways.

INTERNATIONALE
RENT · EXPRESS
ARIS LAUSANNE
STANTINOPLE

This rich culture makes it all the more irritating that railways have been so mucked up in my lifetime. The essential point is that the decision makers consistently miss the point: railways aren't the transport system of the past but of the future. Hardly surprising: these people usually travel the country in ministerial limos. Mrs Thatcher *never* travelled by train, though perhaps for her the phrase 'fellow-traveller' had a more sinister meaning. Railways have come to be seen not as a glory but as an inconvenience and the hapless functionaries of the Department of Transport continue meddling and making worse. This is not what's happening elsewhere. High-speed networks have been built all over the world, despite their cost and consequent subsidies from governments. Why is there such a disparity?

I suppose there's the fact that after the war the shattered infrastructure of Europe had to be rebuilt and countries like France and Germany got into the habit of rolling investment, whereas in Britain we became increasingly influenced by the consumer culture of the US. It's indisputably easier to sell a lifestyle via a motor-car than a train, or maybe I've watched too many episodes of *Mad Men*. But it's surely no accident that together the UK and the US resist the reinvention of the train, while everyone else gets it: railways generate economic growth, allow people to travel quickly and comfortably and cause less environmental damage than the car and plane. They help, in the end, to make societies viable, but our controllers don't see it. But this is merely part of a much bigger collective myopia about our industrial heritage.

I sometimes ponder this as I board a London train in Newcastle's vaulted train shed, gaze at Robert Stephenson's High Level Bridge, then at my fellow passengers, often heading to the capital for meetings at head office. You can see the tension on their faces, as they scan agendas, fingers nervously pecking at company-provided laptops - and on the way home too, as they slump in their seats and order G and T's. They murmur into the mobile – 'Yes love, it went well...' - and you know permission's been granted by the all-powerful for some project or other; or when the warrior returning stares glumly at the commuter towns of Hertfordshire, denied.

I empathise, for I'm in the same boat (if you can be in a boat on a train). After a visit to London with an idea, I too have had the gladiator treatment. I suppose this is what we have now in the North-East – 150 years after the Stephensons changed the world, financed by local investors, we live in what might be called a supplicant economy.

The place of my childhood, a region of shipyards, heavy engineering and coal mines no longer exists. It's an exaggeration to say we don't make anything any more, but not to suggest manufacture is somehow regarded as past its sell-by date. As a result, the region is cleaner, has more amenities, but also a largely de-skilled economy dependent on the public and service sectors. I think we were sold a false prospectus. That makes me angry, because apart from anything else this new economy desperately undervalues the latent skills of the people among whom I live. They've so much to offer, as I know from personal experience. Two members of my own family shared the skill that George Stephenson painstakingly nurtured: the ability to take apart and put back together just about any working mechanism. One great industrialist once told me he believed Geordies possessed what he called 'engineering genes' (though not me, it should be said). It seems such skills are no longer valued in our culture.

The village from which I made my first journey to London in the Coronation year of 1953 no longer has a station of its own. The wooden hut where I sat to watch the trains has gone, so too the works down the line. Shildon wasn't just a stop on Stephenson's Stockton and Darlington Railway, but also the place where those fishy wagons were built. Schools of porpoise and shoals of herring once gathered here but they disappeared when Shildon Shops were closed in the 1980s, along with much of the North's industrial base. In my lifetime, the journey time to the capital from Newcastle has been halved from six hours to three. Despite this, it seems to me in a curious way the distance has grown. Pioneering birthplace of so much technological innovation, the North-East grows ever more remote from power and the people who wield it. There is just one small consolation: the East Coast route is back in public ownership and the London Northern Eastern Railway lives on...

And now the wheels turn and my memory conjures up the Great Railway Journeys of my life. Crossing the vast White Nile 6000 kilometres from the Mediterranean on a grungy train from Nairobi to Kampala. Looking at a shimmering city across the water as our train halts at a red light before the last run into Venezia Santa Lucia. Marking out of 10 the immense grain elevators, gaunt architectural features of the Canadian plains, on the five-day journey from Vancouver to Toronto. Entering the Finland Station in old St Petersburg 80 years after Vladimir Ilyich Lenin arrived in 1917 to foment revolution, though our train wasn't 'sealed'. On the Amtrak South-West Chief from Chicago to LA, climbing the Rockies so slowly at one point Butch and Sundance could have robbed it without recourse to the horse. Two wonderful journeys closer to home, both from Inverness, west to Kyle of Lochalsh and the Isle of Skye, north to Thurso for Orkney. One day I will make these two journeys again from the Central Station, just as I will soon climb the old stone stairs to the Lit and Phil...

Now we approach our final destination and it's time to alight. I am being advised to ensure I have all my baggage with me, cultural and otherwise. I hope I've made my connection and I thank you all for being such considerate fellow passengers.

I sincerely hope you have followed my train of thought.

Newcastle West End Foodbank opened its doors in April 2013 at the Venerable Bede church hall on the West Road to help people who were struggling to provide food for themselves and their families. Poverty is a growing reality for many people in our community and over the years the Foodbank has seen a significant increase in demand for its services and now operates from six satellite centres throughout the city.

COVID-19 has meant that more people are finding it hard to make ends meet. Between January and May 2020 over 20,441 people were beneficiaries of food-parcels issued by the Foodbank, 5,572 of whom were children. In May alone 4,252 people benefited from food-parcels, an increase of 67% on the same period last year and a consequence of the COVID-19 crisis. To meet this rise in demand the Foodbank must secure 21 tons of food every month.

These figures make Newcastle West End Foodbank the country's busiest foodbank and its services are only sustainable with support from our volunteers and donations from the public and local businesses. As COVID-19 continues to affect vulnerable sections of our society we expect demand to remain high. Our Foodbank will continue to work tirelessly to offer a safety net for anyone experiencing food poverty. Your support for our work is deeply appreciated.